My Amazing Toddler Behavioral Series

I Stay Safe.

I Say STOP!

An Affirmation-Themed Book For Toddlers
About Body Safety (Ages 2-4)

By
Suzanne T. Christian

TWO RAVENS
B O O K S

Two Little Ravens
CHILDREN'S NON-FICTION BOOKS

Paperback Edition: 9781964202297
Hardcover Edition: 9781964202303
Digital Edition: 9781964202310

Published in the United States by Two Ravens Books LLC,
254 Chapman Rd, Ste 209, Newark DE 19702

'Expand the mind, free the imagination, one title at a time.'
www.tworavensbooks.com

Welcome to
"I Stay Safe. I Say Stop!"

This book is a delightful collection of easy-to-understand affirmations designed specifically for young children. As you explore its pages together, your child will learn the importance of body safety, personal boundaries, and confidence.

Each page features vibrant illustrations and relatable scenarios, encouraging awareness and open communication. Making this book a regular part of your reading routine can help your toddler understand how to express themselves and stay safe, as repetition is a proven teaching tool.

Prepare for a journey of empowerment, confidence-building, and lots of fun with your toddler!

Suzanne T. Christian

My body is mine;
I keep it safe!

If I don't like tickles. I say, "Stop!"

Hugs are nice,
but **ONLY** when
I want one.

I tell Mommy, Daddy, or Teacher when I need help.

CLAP
CLAP

Hands are for clapping,
not for poking me.
I say, **"Stop!"**

If I don't like it,
I shake my head.
I say, "Stop!"

I am strong;
I can say,
"Leave me alone!"

I tell grown-ups
when I need help.
I stay safe!

If someone wants a hug,
I can give a high-five instead!

My body is special,
and I keep it safe!

If I feel scared,
I tell someone I trust.

When I say "No,"
I mean it!
I say stop!

I am brave;
I can say "No"
anytime!

Listening to my feelings
helps me stay safe.

My body, my rules.
I stay safe!

If someone won't stop,
I shout "No!" louder.

If a touch makes me sad, I tell a grown-up.

When I feel funny inside, I tell Mommy or Daddy.

Even superheroes
need personal space.

My tummy
tells me when
something's
not okay.

Safe touches make me happy.
I stay safe!

I stay safe.
I say, "Stop!"
The End!

My Amazing Toddler Behavioral Series

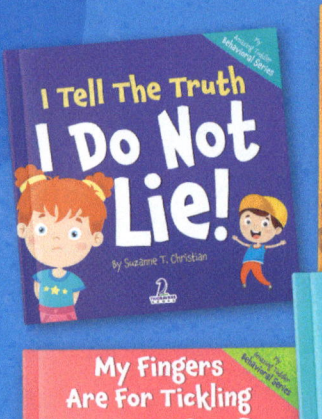

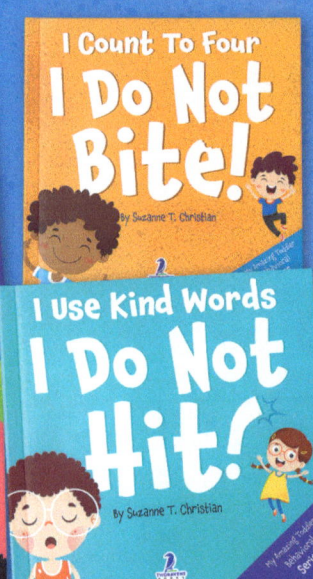

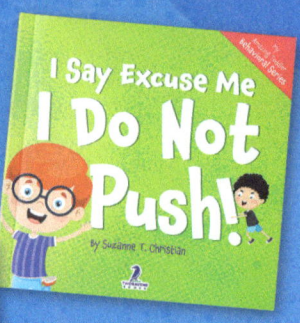

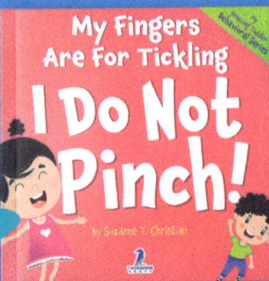

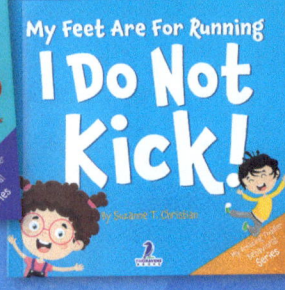

Check Out
Suzanne T. Christian's beloved series
'My Amazing Toddler Behavioral Series'.
Young readers are sure to enjoy!

Two Little Ravens
CHILDREN'S NON-FICTION BOOKS

Dear Amazing Reader,

Thank you for diving into **I Stay Safe. I Say Stop!** with me. If this book touched your heart or made a difference for a young reader, I'd be grateful if you could share your thoughts in a review. Your feedback inspires my future work and helps others discover the magic within these pages.

I'd love to hear from you directly if you have suggestions or ideas for improving the book. Please feel free to reach out to me at **suzanne.christian@tworavensbooks.com.** Your voice counts, and I cherish it deeply.

With heartfelt gratitude,

www.ingramcontent.com/pod-product-compliance
Lightning Source LLC
Chambersburg PA
CBHW041600120626
46551CB00002B/268